MW01620788

hello@littlebookwallah.com

Welcome To The World

On the day you were born,
the moon danced with the stars.

Welcome to the world, little one.

Your incredible journey has only just begun.

The world is wild and wonderful, full of adventure and oh so beautiful.

The world is full of teeny-tiny things

and **enormous** things.

Sweet things,
sour things.

The plants and the flowers are the music of the earth.

All living creatures dance to their rhythm.

The ocean, like life, can be still or calm, rough or rigid—but in the end, always beautiful.

Quite literarily, it's a jungle out there,

and you're going to have
a wild time!

In life, like in the mountains,
everything is in reach.

Just keep climbing.

Snow beautifies everything it covers,

just like kindness.

Wonder,
laughter,

happiness,
and
love
surround you.

Enjoy all the magic as you grow.
These will be the memories you
will hold in your heart forever.

Chase all the bubbles and butterflies.

Jump in
puddles
and dance
in the rain.

Build sandcastles
and swim for
hours.

The little things–they are the BIG things.

May all your wishes come true.

Remember, life is like a rainbow:

You need both rain and sun for its colors to appear.

Don't fear change, for sometimes, in the waves, we find our true direction.

Reach for the stars and believe in you.

No one else is you, and that is your superpower.

Never forget that you are loved

more than words can describe.

Made in the USA
Middletown, DE
05 May 2022

65325470R00022